CALDERA'S DREAM

WRITINGS AND POETRY

ARANYA SEN

XpressPublishing
An imprint of Notion Press

Old No. 38, New No. 6
McNichols Road, Chetpet
Chennai - 600 031

First Published by Notion Press 2019
Copyright © Aranya Sen 2019
All Rights Reserved.

ISBN 978-1-64805-166-1

This book has been published with all efforts taken to make the material error-free after the consent of the author. However, the author and the publisher do not assume and hereby disclaim any liability to any party for any loss, damage, or disruption caused by errors or omissions, whether such errors or omissions result from negligence, accident, or any other cause.

While every effort has been made to avoid any mistake or omission, this publication is being sold on the condition and understanding that neither the author nor the publishers or printers would be liable in any manner to any person by reason of any mistake or omission in this publication or for any action taken or omitted to be taken or advice rendered or accepted on the basis of this work. For any defect in printing or binding the publishers will be liable only to replace the defective copy by another copy of this work then available.

*Dedicated to all who feel like home
and my diary and camera that never complained.*

Contents

Preface   *vii*

1. Caldera — 1
2. Dear Kolkata — 2
3. Traveller's Sigh — 4
4. Homecoming — 5
5. Aurora — 7
6. Dear Thea — 9
7. Brother — 11
8. Paris The Beautiful — 14
9. Christmas Night — 16
10. Santa — 17
11. Denouement — 19
12. Ode To Vincent — 21
13. Thought Of Rain — 22
14. Wabi Sabi — 23
15. Her — 25
16. London — 27
17. Discovering Coldplay — 28
18. Ode To Hawking — 30
19. Calcuttan Suffering — 31
20. Ingénue — 33
21. Felicity Of Love — 35
22. Dear Woman — 36
23. Ode To Pacino — 37

Contents

24. Fabric Of Happenings	38
25. 3am	40
26. Fatima	42
27. Garland Side	43
28. Come Home	44

Preface

My obsession for writing never sprung from innate talent neither from the fascination of books. Though, since the beginning, I was always fascinated by Cinema. Wanted to become a footballer. Now, in pursuit to become a filmmaker yet skeptical about my drive in philosophy, politics, theatrics, drama and public speaking. I hardly appreciated literature, hardly read books till I was 12. Yet, my obsession for writing originated from my need for expression at a time of my own personal traumas and dramas. Few diaries were all to pen down my perspective to universal understandings. I started writing at the age of 13. Since then it has been almost 5 years. This book contains the core of my legible writings and poetry written at the age of 14, 15, 16 and 17. The book's primary ethos is shaped by my expanding thoughts that have developed through age. Some of it was written during heartbreak, some of it during idle thoughts inside gloomy subways, some of it by travelling, some of it in classrooms or while listening to music, some of it was written in hospital beds and the others were written after a beautiful dream. This book is a boy in his youthful years, seeking to dream and to understand a world through his art. Through these years, he has carved three core philosophies for himself and in universal understanding - 1. Caldera - The people, the places or the happenings that keep changing your pursuit and who you are. 2. Thea - The people who stand as pitstops to your earlier life, i.e, after their complete absence, due to their impact, you renew yourself into a another person. 3. Ugestu - an unchanged truth and energy that is always around you placing you in your unerring pursuit in life (it is not god). I strongly believe the concepts of Caldera, Thea and Ugestu are absolute constants that shape the emotional and physical pursuit in anyone's life.

At the brink of adulthood, I am left to live a life that is much bigger than this seemed, and to pen much better than I have penned. However, I have come to an understanding after writing since five years of writing. No matter who you are, where you come from, what your traumas distinctly are, what your morality is made of, what your purpose might seem to be - you and your neighbour and all his neighbour's neighbours are linked by one unerring pursuit - the pursuit of love and happiness.

A Caldera, it's called - a sort of mountain in reverse. A mountain that's had its very heart removed.

— *Cheryl Strayed*

1. Caldera

Oh Caldera, will you ever come home?
Things haven't changed but I'm on my own.

There is a sea of people who go by
Wrinkled faces and workers who sigh.
Caldera, your potrait dies.
Were you lost or were you mine?

My city is always in a race
where people don't love and people don't face.

The sinkholes, Caldera, get wet.
Your grave said "A loving wife"
makes me think of words I wish I hadn't said.

Your son grows without a mother
and this storm in our town comes and goes,
oh Caldera, will you ever come home?

2. Dear Kolkata

Dear Kolkata,

I have almost learned the absolute certainty of beautiful occurring. Nevertheless, I am under the impression that in your vintage world and its beautified retro fashion hidden in labour placards or moving with fine textured individuals of the old and new generation, lies an undeniable truth, I have, peculiarly understood - the simple regard to my place in this world. It is almost vivid yet subtle, how that truth embowers me. A mere gift of an ordinary truth not found in the most extraordinary of cities, which is, I suppose, the most prominent and beautiful irony. For in your halted decades of time, lies the pattern of tramlines that are never straight and the array of typography untouched since the 50s. For if you portray this to a perfectionist or the abundant hypocritical intellectuals in any city of art, they would out-fashion their criticism with the belief that - "A dormant time and progress is a dead city." I strongly do not entertain such arguments for they are, indeed, baseless for a citizen in a city of art. You are, in its truest sense, not a dormant but undying cavalry of a stagnant yet running art. And in this study, I have no intention of flattering you, that is not my definite concern. My concern lies around the sphere of your art and the truth it delivers. I have come to believe and it is certain, no matter the destination I adore or settle for, I will be a hostage for your demand. In you, the demand being immaterial but to articulate it, it is nothing but your art that rests in me. And that truth? It is to create a greater art with the art in me, for the world. It is that nourishing truth that fills my guts. My ordinary extraordinary regard to my place on earth. Thus, if you are invited by sleep or dormancy, these valuable spectrums will remain as real as the midnight ambassadors that illuminate your alleys or the petrichor that fills the saturated reflections of your majesty in collected wet-holes. Do not mistake me, I adore it, for it is so subtly natural as you make it seem to be. Now, if you dare to imagine your artistic deliverance, you must understand that it is kept, only for the esoteric artists and Calcuttans. As I constructed my strong realisation of beautiful occurrings, I should have mentioned that beautiful occurrings may never be understood by the growing crowd that prefers the world of 'Miracles.' Miracles do merely define outstanding unnatural happenings and it is those natural happenings, we forget to beautify. It is only when I am afar from you and your art, does it stand more clearer - A natural scene in a tram that heads to an unknown direction. People strapped, immovable as gradual time flees, letting the tram carry them wherever it desires or the mere strings of broken sunlight that peer through its window lines, touching the smiling and the pale faces. I have happened to love that world as beautiful as it is, moving and stagnant. This is a world I'll be believing in, timeless and beautiful.

3. Traveller's Sigh

The dumb concious of
every human lie here.
Under the mountains
where the monast hums
where every thought
is a blessing
every hour
is a spark of solitude
every minute is cry
of a story

It has been hitting me for a while
of uneven tempts and soft winds
and the common cold where the leaves fall by

I venture to this mountain now
of every dream and stop
I do not wish anyone
goodnight.

4. Homecoming

Spending two years afar, maybe this is what I've learned. I've understood it sitting amidst the calm of home and leaving amidst the chaos of departure. As flights take off and come back home in busy airports, in the wind of joy and breath of sorrow, I have found my answer. There is no boy who doesn't wish to be a man. To leave the touch of home, a family, and heartwarming friends. And maybe that is the music we are all searching for. The music when you're away in an unknown, young city, listening to the blurry street lights chase your song at 3AM, while you cross the road on a winter night and you wonder how beautiful it is to be alone. When you're feeling the wind that sings in cadence through your window pane. Isolation stands as the only growth and beauty to you. Your friends become a memory and you mistake the everyday caregivers in this new place as your friend. You succeed far greater and understand far greater. You are part of a world that doesn't call you its own but you have to grow your roots and water the art here. Call it another home. But the truth is, or perhaps the truth I have discovered, searching and searching. In a small town, the weary cat wonders on rooftops spending nights away from her kittens. In her return to them, you will find a heart of an animal that doesn't want to leave that moment and place. And in the same way, the homeless man on cobbled streets has his home too. There the home lies beside the man in the body and soul of a small puppy. His heart graces the dog on a cold night to keep him as warm as summer life. And even in the mountain zephyr, where a traveller stands looking at Alaskan highlands, he wishes his family would be here with him, feeling the wind as he did, living. And there is a boy, sitting in his room writing this while listening to a music mellow to his heart. His trophies, his achievements, his leadership, his legacy here means nothing to him in a place he can't call home. It is almost as beautiful as it strikes him, that nothing can replace the warmth within the doors of his heart where there are friends who have shaped his art since years and a family who has never left.

5. Aurora

When I look at you
I see waves caressing the shore
and sunlight sneaking
through the trees

I hear your voice
it is a bird singing in the morning
and the laughter of old friends

I can see your eyes
as the warmth of a gentle bonfire
and the subtle summer breeze

I can feel your hair moving gently
with the grey dead skies and
stormy country winds

I can feel your hand on mine
changing the gear of the car
that drives through
endless sunset meadows

I can see you walking

inside a gloomy and wet subway
disappearing with every onboard train

You're not there anymore
but it feels as if you're
everywhere

6. Dear Thea

Dear Thea,

It's been raining beautifully in Kolkata when the year's just barely begun and I've been sitting, in newer breezes of life listening to the ambassadors cross wet roads and remembering you when you taught me what 'petrichor' meant. I've never loved the rain more, since then. I've been remembering the time when your home was just an Uber ride away to a beautiful terrace of windy country skies. I've been remembering the days when all you could do when I smiled was call me an idiot and refuse to kiss me. I've been remembering your realest heart that lasted with phone calls longer than 11 hours. In you, I remember, a girl that grew a beautiful human being empowered by her beliefs and a heart that had so much love purer than the ideal. I remember a boy who could never reciprocate any of it, because of his rudimentary, arrogant and immature state. But your love remained there throughout each conflict, as a best friend and as a lover. In the 3 years without you, I have not loved neither tried loving anyone as much as I have loved you. For all you were, in a world with plastic people, a breathing example of a real persona of love and kindness. I've been wondering often about the truth in a certain question I have been asking myself since these 3 years - whether it is alright to love someone when they're gone? In truth, I will never know but in my ideals I have discovered, it is natural and right to love someone even when they cease to be in your world. Loving you never meant ceasing my living, it meant inspiring every heart of it. While looking at the many hued palette sky listening to James Bay when I wondered what the hell is my purpose, I have loved you. Sitting by unknown avenues in benches with a pen and a diary to fill, I have loved you. But the reason, I wrote this, Thea, was to remind myself the intricate beauty of you in my heart but understand the greater light in letting you go. As the year begins and it rains the third year without you, I make a paper boat, fill it with my past of misdoings and sail it into a puddle with your soft hands. As it sails away, I let you go to your own world of love thinking my world of love will once again, come too.

7. Brother

Brother
you burned the last violin
to keep us warm
there was no music that night
just you and me looking at the city turn blue
and the distant lights became dormant for a while
you would tell me about your sinister exploits
but
cry a flood by the afternoon
over a girl you once loved
And I would listen
As age dawned
so did the doors to your room close to family
I felt like knocking
but I never did
envious of your world
in a castle of friendship
saddened by my world and emotions
in bars
and winter came,
so did the longer nights
"Dada, there is good jazz in Bombay"

I told you before you left.
I have been here,
at home for a while,
in a maddening growth of who the saviour
was only me
walking around the junction at night
resting in a broken city
watching the traffic blur my future
until the dawn hits
But don't worry,
this life without a mother
still serves us goodness
And Summer did come
it broke down the family
I would wish to see you
so I would stay awake
and wonder how your struggles
might perhaps be
turning my struggles a bit less painful
It's odd you know
As much as I like my city
The people
The waste of times of ourselves
The cacophonies
The art
It is in a similar liking

I wish to grow out of
and leave
You must be at Ray's now
getting a pizza for yourself
smoking ciggarattes with your another
gripped on a ride back to your home
tearing the strings from your broken guitar
Tell me Brother
Do I scare you like our mother?
Or do you still love me the same.

8. Paris The Beautiful

As winter winds mark an art in the Parisian life, the summer baked aroma is replaced with fragrant chariàds and rosès. The red haired woman named Jeanne gathers her morning flowers from the station beside Lyon and another soul, quite with the charisma and the never dying-ness named Seine, watches her reflection as she plays with his frosty water. In another alley, one clanging cycle passes through a cobbled wet hole, into a neighbourhood that is so busy in the making of a jolly Christmas feast.

It is, I admit, too hard to understand the miracle of love and life that shapes a city, but however, it is never the same when you are in Paris. Love here is like a turning road that takes you round and round to beautiful places and life is in the person who is driving there. Simply, it is a maddening world we live in today, but if you ever find yourself in Mont Valerià n on a winter midnight, overlooking Paris as men and women gather the streets, with the warmth enough to spark the city lights and the golden saxophones and keys that strike a silver jazz note and in that moment you'll know that you are in the process of having a maddening feast. As for me, I am here, trying to grasp the thought of Paris's loveliness, its midnight breath and its undying music.

There is only a soul in the hill, gazing at the distant lights that reflect within him. There is a bottle of Margaux and two glasses. I reach my hand towards the Vinyl player and adjust a familiar song. "La Vie En Rose". As a peaceful note absorbs me, I glance at a world that is filled with the season's peace, joy and its greetings. A family gathers over a sensational dinner, folding their hands together, praying in peace as the light shines over their home. Two lovers run near the tower and kiss their soul while the snow falls off the sparkling street-lamps.

I pour myself an elegant sum of wine. I pour the other, with the vibrant and beautiful thought that keeps me living - that one day she would return, sit beside me with her radiant smile as I would wrap my arms around her. We would drink our youthful hearts out till Paris turned ever more beautiful.

9. Christmas Night

It is the cake spilled
Where no one remembered it was your day
but I did.
Frosting sweet of Christmas days
Sneared into the strands of your hair
When it was to be your prettiest day.

10. Santa

You're rather too young when you realise the reality of Santa Claus. The idea of him isn't hidden in his existence or perhaps, simply bearing gifts. It's the universal acceptance of a feeling we are in so pursuit of - it's sooner you realise Santa Claus is - Happiness. The cadence of the jingle bells and the beautiful fragrance of fresher days or the sight of a winter delight or simply the magical cry of the city you live in. I've come to realise that everything is a gift. Even the better smile of your mother or the laugh of your old friend - it's perhaps people that are gifts to your life. It's the door bell ringing to welcome childhood's soulmate who you've played video games with, in screens and settled serious football scores in the field. Who you have loved more than a brother and who has remembered to love you back when you forgot to care about him. It's that little person who has kept your secret of a sacred barbie scale you once kept hidden with you, fearing that the world has set codes for a man. It's the loved one, who wouldn't tell you who her crush is. It's the female brother, who has got your back in the world of security and dance, but who can smack you the hardest in your balls. It's eating and drinking your heart out for a Christmas to be Christmassy and where better than 'Park Street'? And then, tucked in a small nostalgic and a better world in golf green, is a childhood friend met after a decade, who resembles you and your roots more than you resemble yourself. It's time wishing you beautiful circles and happenings. Somewhere between all of this is a Santa that exists - Happiness. A strong and a beautiful feeling that you matter and that life is in fact, peculiarly, beautiful.

11. Denouement

There is an earth in the truth we pursue - she is found escaping the heart of young cities, listening to mellow Hozier at empty midnight churches, where religion would call music its candidate for hope. She is found at the spark of laughter in a familiar call of home at a dinner-table ready for Christmas and set to see its young souls become taller than the Christmas tree, through the beautiful years.

In a few magical degrees, you will find her in the moonlight, perfecting a delight in the course of the night brooks and rivers, as they travel through salmon terrains and forests of life. Look closer, she is there lying plain inside a hospital room at 6th street, just above love and just below heaven. She smiles a last breathe as the old man holds her old hands, counting memories till it's new year.

You will find her sitting chilled and reddened by the winter winds of the city of life. On the Avenue bench, she leaves a letter, perhaps for her father who never returned or her lover that never fancied her wild and egotistical spirit. You will find her song in the fragrant wood-dust Jewish piano as it plays the cries of a summer desire in azure skies.

That earth, that truth, is everywhere. Everywhere, we so beautifully observe and listen to, as a truthful song.

Today, we need to validate the earth of it, understand the simple undying truth and then tomorrow - We will live, beautifully.

12. Ode To Vincent

Do you see, the field where the crows fly to the north
with the strokes to kill war
The fishermen in the stream
that enjoy the cheap alcohol
and the boats that become the water in the tide

The night lights that illude the village
with its blurry rage
in beauty and in strength
the stars in the starry sky

A depth of colour and waves
the portrait of the morning postmen
and the lovely men

The sunflowers that are the sun
and the detailed intricate being in the normal world

With it waves, impression and colour
that destroys the cold wind of the genius

He is a man. He is art. He is magic.
He is Vincent.

13. Thought Of Rain

It's raining. I have just discontinued an 18 minute stare out of the window. There are soft, cold winds amidst still sounds of gossip. Morning classroom conversations have sprouted after a lecture that introduced stoicism in literature. I stretch my sight to the wide and wider grey clouds and the hills that possess less greener hues than before. There is a pain. A hurt. I am far away from home. There's a thought of Van Gogh in almost no presumption, in how immaculately he captured the unseen waves of colour in a normally discoloured world. To distinct the unique of the normal has been the essence the artistry. The raindrops start trickling with no newer drops that follow. The rain must be departing. There is a feeling of home. I am home now. My father is here, he rests in his room. My beloved mother watches over me from the heaven above the pitch monsoon skies. I can hear the work of my city. There is a loud thunder. The wind-chime suddenly stops. I am awake. The gossips continue. It is still raining. The sound of doors click. Our lecturer walks in. I close the windows with one thought - I wish my art comes back and my family is safe, happy and loved.

14. Wabi Sabi

The power of language lies in its subtle beauty of description and articulation. No language in the world, no matter how beautiful and intriguing, can describe every aspect and feeling of human and natural life. But if one learns all languages in the world, he'll open up a pattern of endless understanding and definitions. Today, we're on the ardent march of being innovative and discovering new sciences and newer spaces. We forget how beautiful it is, to firstly understand ourselves and our elements. There is so much of beauty in learning a language. You don't just learn newer words, you learn a newer understanding of life. Today, I came across a beautiful Japanese phrase, very common and heard all over - わび さび (wabi sabi) - this phrase translates to two beautiful meanings, when intertwined, it forms a greater one. Wabi, means desolation and loneliness and Sabi means to wither away with the beauty of passing time. I think that's where we go wrong. We mistake agony and sadness to be a signature of a fullstop or a distinct pause in our lives. However, agony and pain and suffering, are very distinct and beautiful things. They allow you to stop and look, admire the little things, grant you a larger breath and an even larger art. Sorrow and suffering gives you an ink to paint an open canvas. When you're finally the artist of your sorrow, you create and understand things, many have never understood before. Japanese is very mesmerising as a language but more than that, every language have their beautiful phrases. My language - Bengali, has so many. Now, before you delve into an entire world filled with curiosity, engage all of it in understanding the life in yourself and not in what's around you. That way, the world will have a beautiful understanding.

15. Her

After her, the world has been a breeze of realities. Realities, I perhaps wasn't ready for. Realities I haven't gathered the earth of. I started by saying it was a 'breeze' as the unfurling of it was in fact, strongly harsh but later, the most beautiful. Painted skies were replaced with uncertain and stormy ends. Home replaced itself with an environment highly alien and unnatural for my kind. However, in all of it, I haven't lost my pursuit for a love, simple and profound and an almost ordinary youth. I am aware, that with each breeze, I am anew and renewing, of which the good and bad, I'm unaware of. Unaware yet pretending, it is in fact the good. After her, I have perhaps reconsidered my dreams yet it is real than ever. I have found her essence in every truth I understand and in every art I pursue. And if it is the sound of love, so be it. If it is merely a spark of her muse, so be it. What is so deeply natural will always be — After her, I have attended a world in sanctuary, realising every pattern to mark and every flaw to heal.

Uncertain skies will remain, stormy ends may never end, unnatural happenings may become natural but what's definite will be definite — After her, it's a world I am starting to understand. An art that is not gifted but is discovered in struggle.

After her, it is yet another life, living.

16. London

Somewhere between the Thames and streets of Leicester
I left my heart
Across the midnight drinks
Where old friends made old friends
Who couldn't wish for the night to be better
Where the city sang a song
Which made empires weak
Which ran across the tube - undefined, majestic
London was thunder!

17. Discovering Coldplay

It was in hearing the tunes of a song, that echoed from my elder brother's room from the 34th floor to the window in my room on the 35th. It was in seeing my father trying to reciprocate the cinematic elements of a video in rewind using me as the actor and my brother, editing the video. It was in being captivated by the music of the man who just jumped up from a pillow and started walking backwards in a world that ironically, never stops moving forward. And yet as beautiful as it was, so was the heart in a song that I had never felt before, as the man sung his ways driving back the love of his life. It was sneaking into my brothers room as he played the songs of the band in every morning and midnight delight. It was when dad gifted my first pad, music was no longer a beholder of two in the family - I had music with me too. It was listening to the call of a king in France and a tune that sung freedom and happiness. The drumbeats made my heart turn wilder and the pace of time grew more beautiful. It was running back home in heavy Calcuttan rain, after schooldays of pace and bustle and when the school rang, I ran, drenched in rain yet eager to fill the ears with familiar music. It was growing up, surreally with a torn family yet finding a world beautifully, in wet football fields, the cities magic, young love and friends. It was growing up replacing pencils with cigarettes and paper boats with cameras and small drums with bigger band instruments. It was however, with a timeline and beauty of their music, throughout. It was being stranded inside school in rain, playing their music with my best friend in auditoriums and musical classes to keep us breathing, when no one knew what their music was. It was the first time, I took up the mike and sang "When you try your best but you don't succeed..." with a senior on our Annual day. It was 3ams, when the music of a runaway elephant rang greater beats than any other. It was a trip to Europe and London after which the meaning of the music took colours of beautiful avenues. Through all of this, I have lived, loved and moved with a time that began in that very first spark in my elder brother's room - Discovering Coldplay.

18. Ode to Hawking

The quantum world.
A beauty.
That understood
the unknown.
And the quantum man
who spoke
the language.
And the god
is dead.
Love is born.
Rest now.
The cosmos smiles.

19. Calcuttan Suffering

It was months after the wet rains flooded Calcutta, with its furious and beautiful glory. As the men ran to shelter, the real gold, however, stood in feeling the city's rain as it reflected the colours and cacophony that so moved the breeze, water and life their. The youngest child chased the cat. The customary shops men lifted his rusted door and a mother cooked fresh food for her child who was still dreaming a life without school. Somewhere amidst the broken corners of the alleys, the call for Namaz had started. It took an exhilarating form as it spread an echo, forming ripples in the cities wet holes. The Rickshaws now parked itself at the junctions. In it awestrucking majesty, it had made a painting of itself in the wet vintageness of the monsoon world. Allah touched the street mosques, Kali had blessed the land and Jesus sang to the hymns of the churches. The city was never made out of its everyday life. It was born out of the stories and the whispers of the grandfathers and grandmothers who rested in the creak-chairs and designed the way to an artful generation. It was born out of the wayfarers that left their earthen impression. Some, in the ceiling of trams. Some, in the the dirt of the architectural alleys and some, in the call of the old morning postmen. I started walking through the breeze in the silent neighbourhoods as I understood a world, I had never understood before. This city was more than beautiful. It was the smell of earth after the rain and the summer sorrow of the sky. It was the pattern of coloured hues. It was the fuel to my dreams and the comfort to my thoughts. And as long she is in me, I cannot say I'm suffering.

20. Ingénue

There is no definition
for the feeling I get in my dream
when she smiles in her sleep

It is no poetry neither is it fate
When you walk across the avenue
where people sell their dreams
 where people buy their dreams
They are alive.
I am not.

I'm the dead that walks
admiring hitler and painted ceilings
The oddly refreshing darkness.
The beautiful catastrophe.
I don't regret the fact,
but in fact,
I thank her for locating me
somewhere between
old fascination and the bloody madness

Even when I try to sleep,

rub my head
when I fall sick,
I look out my window
when the lights blurred
when you were no longer beautiful.

The high trills,
the post lights,
the mess,
how you read no poetry made you so weak.
Love was weak.
You told me something
in that morning fiasco
it was like the last words of the woman in my dreams
The words were so many yet I remember one.
"You're my favourite candidate in love"

For once you lied, you bastard.

21. Felicity of Love

I still remember the days when this city would rain through its pouring heart. It would cover the skies so long as not even God could lay his eyes on it.

You could sit down, write a dampen diary, or cry your heart out. It was like a dream. Calcutta was a dream and I was in love with someone.

How much the agony inside me then turned into beautiful drops of rain. It trickled its way through our pages and gave our story a song. I loved her. I loved her with all my heart.

And I miss her even more today, at a time when there are none beside me, watching the city rain again.

22. Dear Woman

Dear Woman
of gentle air
battles wars
that are not fair

at night
she lets her wet jeans and dreams dry

Tell me dear woman
do you smile
or do you cry?

23. Ode to Pacino

In person, he does not disappoint. He seduces. Call me Al. Here's my cell number. A kiss on each cheek. Everything, except his physical stature, is outsize. His skin is tanned the colour of cognac; the hair a tempest. His voice, a Bronx rasp, shades the world in italics. Where Robert De Niro recedes in public appearances, all nods and mumbles, Pacino offers a banquet of observations. Pacino is sipping tea, surrounded by hounds, in front of his white-columned house in this fabled, palm-lined enclave. He's at ease, but he doesn't fit, an inveterate New Yorker in a far too sunny place. Buses loiter on his block every few minutes, tourists trying to steal a glimpse beyond the gates of the man whom film historian David Thomson in 2002 deemed "our greatest actor now." Pacino is the winner of an Oscar (eight nominations), two Tonys, two Emmys, four Golden Globes (17 nominations), a National Medal of Arts and the AFI life achievement. Pacino long ago proved the studio brass wrong, that he's the furthest thing from a disaster.

"You gotta realize yourself in all your roles. For me, the acting is very much a sanctuary," he says. "It's a place where I go and feel as close to what I should be doing in life, and why I'm here."

And so he acts, constantly.

24. Fabric of Happenings

I know not how far this is
of where I lie
writing
every truth
I'm yet to scar

This was never
a call of god
A disturbed Eve
or her apple
It was the wisdom
flying in the wind
moving
our growth
your growth
in an ordinary world
with ordinary love

No matter how far I am
how far I'll ever be
I will build sanctuaries
of newer love
found in alleyways and songs

and her morning smile
newer people
in every crossroad
with idealism and dreams
and newer landscapes
that water and touch the grass
of every heart

This is my happening
This is where I'll be
and always be
going.

25. 3AM

In the temple we prayed
of holocaust midnight
across our timely city
where you were not with me tonight

the scent of a dreaming woman
smelled earth in the soil of tantrum
the rhythm made us wait
wishing for the rain's anthem

We go back and run forth
we do not wait for our unbroken smile
and in that chair, the rolling one
our faqira had cried

Our town is no more the same
the cabs work no more
the engines stop working
the cars reach the shore

I wish to go back to the time
the city was alive
not the songs and the chaos

of the crows and dogs at night

At 3:00 AM,
it feels like an apocalypse hit home
you and me
we've all grown.

26. Fatima

The sea felt the tides
with the ones who left home
broken, petrified
of alien cacophony
Fatima wept
Why wouldn't she?
They took away all her heart
that needed a home
Fatima will never die
will never peer
at what's behind her
A burned, tormented
world
Yesterday, I saw her
at the harbour
blue eyes as the ocean
in a night sky
when the other world
slept
11PM
She wondered with the wind
if her world was but a dirty trick
she never wished for

27. Garland Side

In the moving trailers of time
youth is the sudden heart
the boy's illusive eyes
coloured the cry from the start

Who was the boy when his father left?
fatherless?
watered hs fears in tears
made the foe his lover
and the one without a mother
the one magic of a dear

in a deck far from home
he wishes time another goodbye
that when december's sorrow is not his own
there lies a friend
waiting on the garland side

28. Come Home

The glistening sun sets drowning itself in the small fields of kolkata. Leaving a silhouette of the tamarind tress, humming winds and chirping crickets that play in a symphony for the evening. The bikers ride, and we finish our last game of bat and ball. Lost every game but won each time. While the small newborn kittens that haven't opened their soft eyes, cuddle themselves in the search for an evenings brunch, the aroma of fresh herbs and rice spread through the frontyards. A woman's footstep are heard, that travels through the door houses of older calcutta. With an old muslin apron of worked fabric, tying her hair with a wooden clip, my mother opens the rusted windows of the kitchen. She smiles.

"Buno, come home".